ANIMAL HEROES

SUPERSQUADS!

Able to capture prey with a single squirt . . .

cowritten by
HEATHER LANG and **JAMIE HARPER**

illustrated by **JAMIE HARPER**

CANDLEWICK PRESS

Introducing . . . the most talented teams in the wild!
No challenge is too great for these heroes to face.
Their mission: to survive and thrive.

Some teams are big; others are small. Some are made up
of youngsters; others are led by moms or dads or grannies!

They're friends.

They're families.

They're communities.

They're **SUPERSQUADS!**

What's the secret to their success?

COMMUNICATION!

Animals use lots of creative methods to share information with teammates and to signal a call to action.

Grooming is the language of love in a snow monkey troop. It helps them to form tight bonds, reduce stress, and communicate affection. Plus, a good cleaning never hurts.

DANGER!
DANGER!

chick-a-dee-dee-dee

When a predator is near, a chickadee warns the flock by using a variety of calls depending on the threat level.

More "dee, dee, dees" at the end of the call means more danger.

chick-a-dee-dee-dee-dee-dee

chick-a-dee-dee-dee-dee-dee-dee-dee-dee-dee-dee-dee-dee-dee-dee

Movin' and groovin' . . . A honeybee dances, communicating to hive mates where they can find food. The dance moves share information about the direction and location of the food source. If it's top quality, the bee will really rock 'n' roll.

Look at his moves!

Look at his clues!

It's the round dance!

Food must be close.

Let's GO!

You should be dancing!

WHIZZZZZ

A super teammate is dedicated and will step up to lead the squad when needed, even if it means making sacrifices or taking risks.

When spiny lobsters hightail it to warmer waters, they take turns at the front of the line. The leader navigates, pushing through the water and blocking the current for the lobsters behind. This makes the long trek easier and faster.

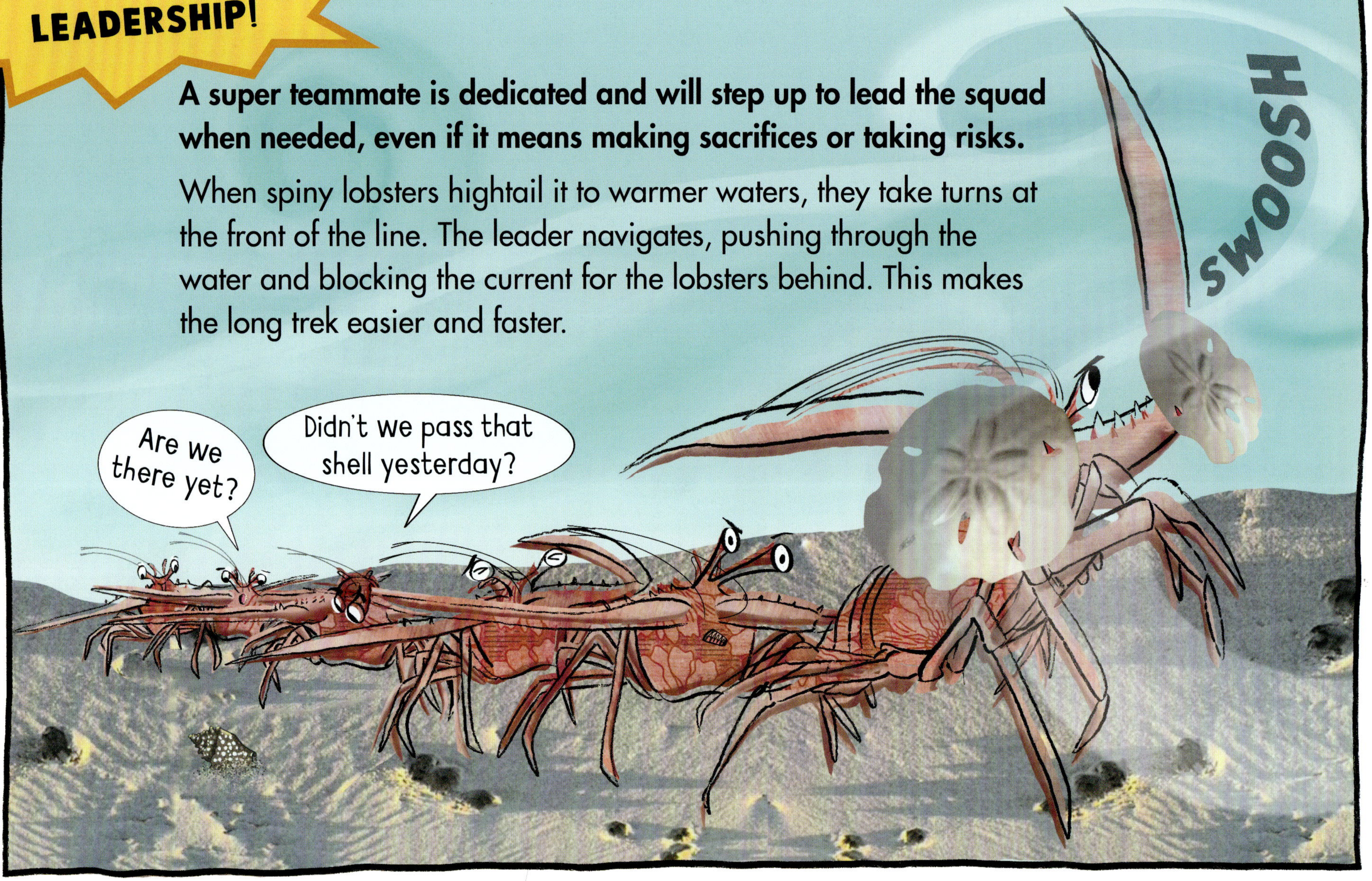

Three cheers for orca matriarchs! The oldest female orca, often a granny, leads and protects the pod. She teaches the youngsters how to find and catch food, even on land. It takes lots of training.

Dividing up and sharing tasks can help a supersquad be super successful. Every animal has an important role to play.

Millions of leaf-cutter ants work together to grow fungus gardens: food for the colony. From tending the gardens to harvesting leaf pieces to defending the nest, an ant's job depends on its size.

TEAM LEAF-CUTTER

QUEEN

SOLDIER

LARGE FORAGER

TRASH COLLECTOR

FUNGUS GARDENER

NANNY

Naked mole rats line up to dig their burrow and find food underground. The front rat digs with its chisel-like teeth, "sweepers" kick the dirt backward, and the last rat blasts the soil up and out of the hole.

Wait . . . we're naked?

We've got hair between our toes . . .

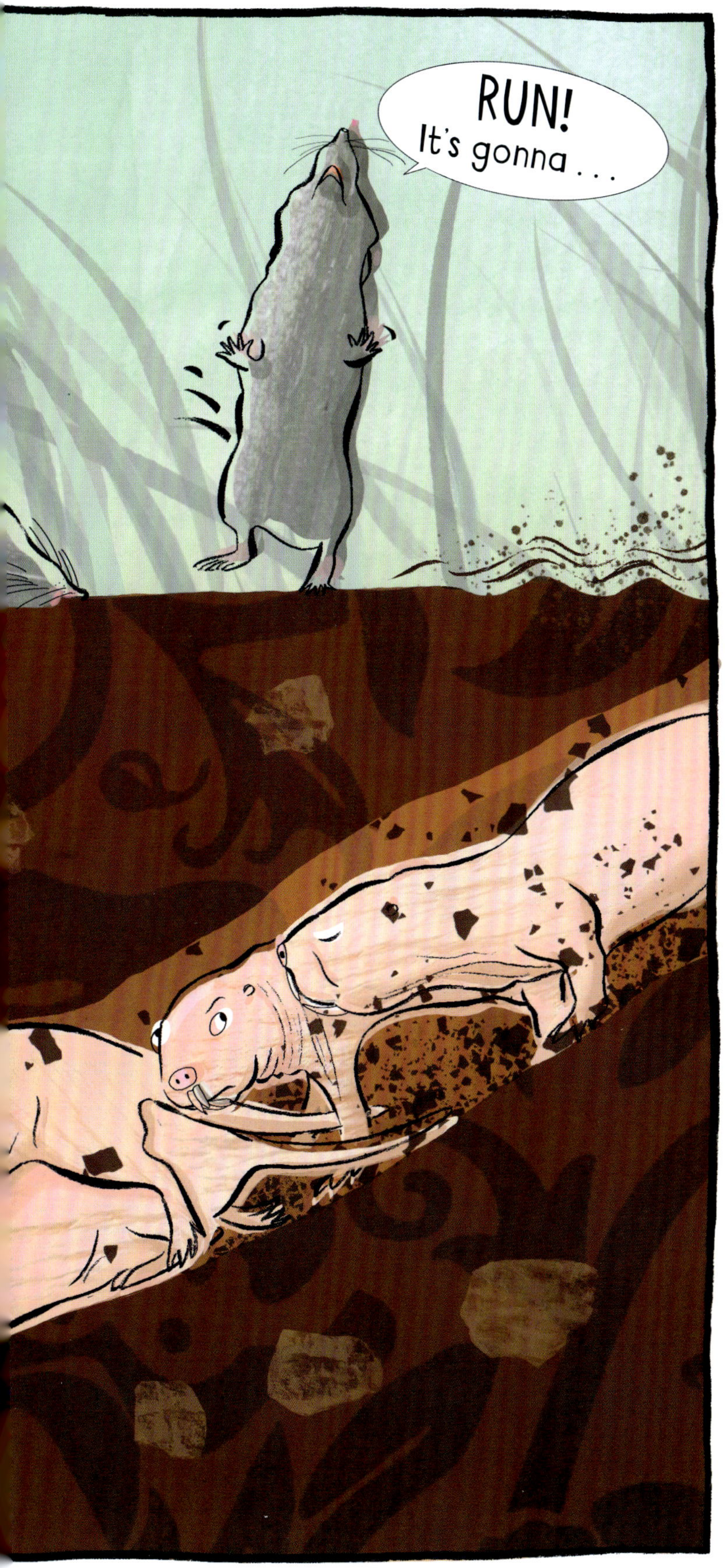
RUN!
It's gonna . . .

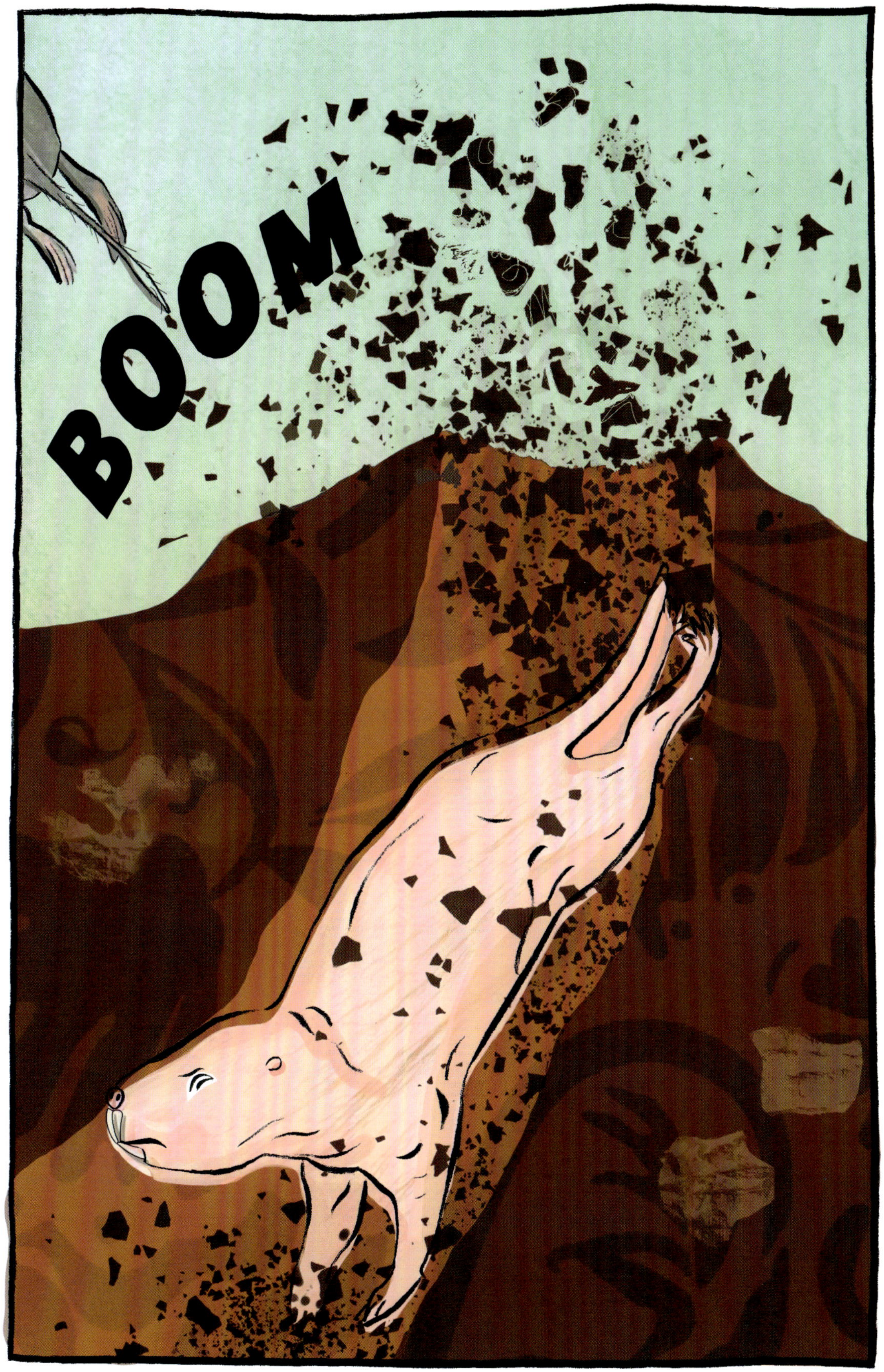
BOOM

It's all teeth on deck for a busy beaver squad. The whole family chips in to build a dam, construct a lodge, stash food for the winter, and babysit the kits.
I'm fixing the roof. What about you?
Food shopping.
LODGE SWEET LODGE
On patrol, ma'am!
I'm with Mom.
Babysitter?!
ha ha
BOO
hee-hee

We need mud. Can you go?
Rock, paper, scissors . . .

I need a shopping cart.

hee-hee

Mom said NO SWIMMING!

ha ha

DIVERSITY!

When two species embrace their differences and partner up, they're better together. This is called mutualism.

Ostriches and zebras have each other's backs. The ostrich's keen eyesight combined with the zebra's excellent sense of smell and hearing creates a strong defense against hungry predators. What a team!

Sometimes it just takes two to make a supersquad. A sea anemone uses its stinging tentacles to protect a hermit crab and, in return, enjoys free rides and tasty tidbits from the crab.

Nice hat, Nora!

I know. It's all the rage.

I love leftovers.

MUNCH MUNCH MUNCH

Danger ahead!

I've got you covered.

A moray eel and a cleaner shrimp make a dynamic duo. The eel opens its mouth so the shrimp can nibble on parasites—a meal for the shrimp and a free cleaning for the eel.

Looks like a busy day.

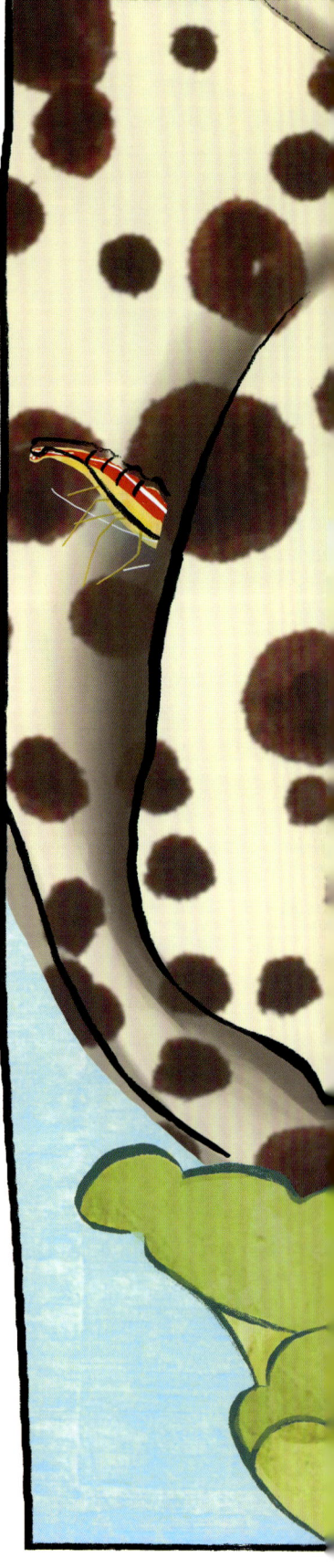

Alone they are great; together they are unbeatable! Often, members of a supersquad work in unison to achieve a common goal. A bigger squad can mean a bigger success.

For starlings, there's safety in numbers. Hundreds of thousands fly in a synchronized ballet: swirling, soaring, dipping, and diving in cloudlike formations across the sky. This makes it very challenging for a hungry predator, like a falcon, to lock in on a target.

Animals are never too young to join a supersquad. When king penguin parents go off to find food, they might leave their chick for several months . . . YIKES! To keep warm and stay safe from predators, hundreds of chicks huddle together in "nurseries" called crèches.

Move over, Spidey—there's a new "web-shooter" in town. Velvet worms band together to hunt, shooting sticky slime to trap their prey.

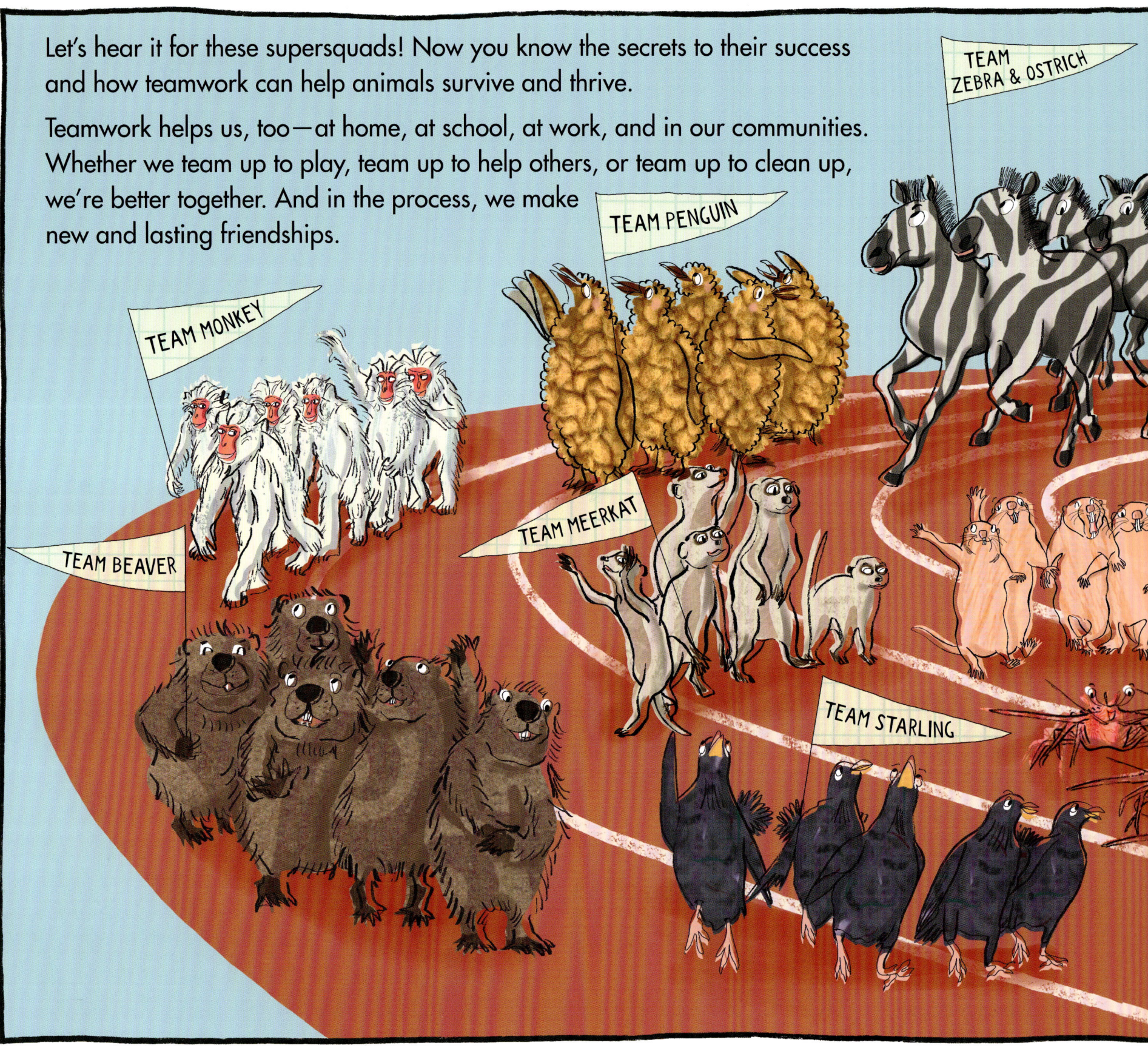

Let's hear it for these supersquads! Now you know the secrets to their success and how teamwork can help animals survive and thrive.

Teamwork helps us, too—at home, at school, at work, and in our communities. Whether we team up to play, team up to help others, or team up to clean up, we're better together. And in the process, we make new and lasting friendships.

TEAM ZEBRA & OSTRICH

TEAM PENGUIN

TEAM MONKEY

TEAM BEAVER

TEAM MEERKAT

TEAM STARLING

Who's on your squad?
And what makes it SUPER?

CHICKADEE
SUPER VOCAL

MY SQUAD IS CALLED a banditry or flock. **I LIVE** in the forests, fields, parks, and cities of North America, and **I EAT** seeds, berries, insects, and invertebrates.

GUESS WHAT? To announce that a fast predator is flying toward us, I make a high-pitched "seet" call to warn the flock.

HONEYBEE
SUPER EXPRESSIVE

Check out my sweet moves!

MY SQUAD IS CALLED a hive or swarm. **I LIVE** in gardens, woodlands, orchards, and meadows, and **I EAT** nectar, pollen, and honey.

GUESS WHAT? When I dance, I share the smell of a flower with my hive mates. They take a whiff and a taste with their antennae.

SNOW MONKEY
SUPER SOCIAL

MY SQUAD IS CALLED a troop. **I LIVE** in warm and cool forests in Japan, and **I EAT** fruit, berries, seeds, insects, crabs, and bird eggs.

GUESS WHAT? In the frigid winter, I rely on my thick fur, and I like to soak in the hot springs and snuggle with my troop.

SPINY LOBSTER
SUPER COOPERATIVE

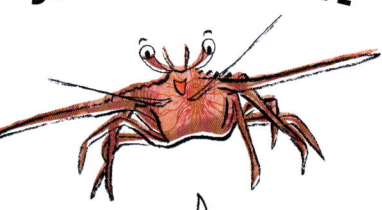

MY SQUAD IS CALLED a pod. **I LIVE** in rock crevices and coral reefs, and **I EAT** crabs, clams, and other invertebrates.

GUESS WHAT? When threatened, we defend ourselves by forming a circle with our spines pointing outward.

MEERKAT
SUPER RESPONSIBLE

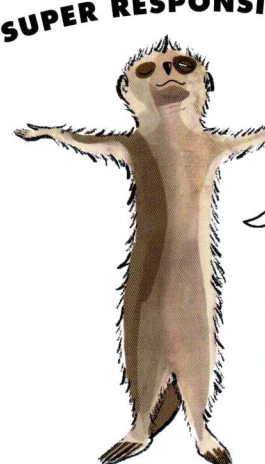

MY SQUAD IS CALLED a mob. **I LIVE** in deserts and grasslands in the southern tip of Africa, and **I EAT** beetles, spiders, scorpions, small reptiles, eggs, fruit, and plants.

GUESS WHAT? I teach youngsters how to hunt scorpions by bringing them injured ones for practice.

ORCA
SUPER CONNECTED

MY SQUAD IS CALLED a pod. **I LIVE** in oceans all over the world, and **I EAT** fish, walruses, seals, penguins, sharks, and other whales.

GUESS WHAT? I live with my family for life—mothers with sons, daughters, and daughters' offspring. We communicate with our own set of clicks and whistles.

LEAF-CUTTER ANT
SUPER ORGANIZED

MY SQUAD IS CALLED an army or a colony. **I LIVE** on the forest floor in underground nests, and **I EAT** fungus.

GUESS WHAT? I release scents, called pheromones, from my body to mark trails and communicate with other ants.

NAKED MOLE RAT
SUPER EFFICIENT

YES, poop—it's organic!

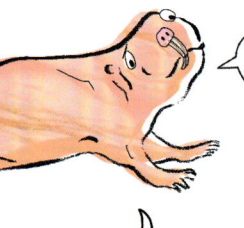

MY SQUAD IS CALLED a colony. **I LIVE** in burrows in East Africa, and **I EAT** underground roots and plant material, and sometimes my own poop.

GUESS WHAT? My lips close behind my teeth, so I can dig without getting dirt in my mouth.

MY SQUAD IS CALLED a colony. **I LIVE** in ponds, rivers, marshes, streams, and wetlands, and **I EAT** leaves, woody stems, and aquatic plants.

GUESS WHAT? I help keep my lodge safe and cozy with multiple underwater entrances and a floor covered with wood shavings.

BEAVER
SUPER BUSY

SEA ANEMONE
SUPER DEFENSIVE

I **LIVE** in all marine habitats, and **I EAT** tiny fish, crabs, and plankton.

GUESS WHAT? When an animal touches me, I fire a tiny "harpoon," which injects venom into the predator or prey.

HERMIT CRAB
SUPER INGENIOUS

I **LIVE** in coral reefs and intertidal zones, and **I EAT** small fish and invertebrates such as worms or plankton.

GUESS WHAT? As I grow, I move into larger shells, and sometimes I bring my sea anemone with me.

OSTRICH
SUPER SUPERSIZED

MY SQUAD IS CALLED a flock or herd. I **LIVE** in the grasslands and savannas of Africa, and **I EAT** most leafy plants and fruits and sometimes insects, lizards, and snakes.

GUESS WHAT? I am the largest bird, and I have the largest eyes of any land animal. I also lay the biggest eggs—each is about the size of 24 chicken eggs.

ZEBRA
SUPER STRATEGIC

MY SQUAD IS CALLED a herd. **I LIVE** in the grasslands and savannas of Africa, and **I EAT** grass.

GUESS WHAT? When we're in a group, sometimes called a dazzle, our stripes blend, making it difficult for predators to pick out an individual to attack.

MORAY EEL
SUPER SCARY

I **LIVE** in reefs, tidal pools, sandy habitats, and seagrass beds, and **I EAT** fish, crustaceans, squid, and octopus.

GUESS WHAT? I have a flexible jaw that opens wide. I can swallow prey whole.

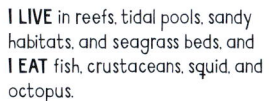

Can you fit me in for a cleaning?

CLEANER SHRIMP
SUPER BRAVE

You bet!

I **LIVE** in coral reefs, caves, crevices, and tidal pools, and **I EAT** parasites, dead tissue, leftover food, and small invertebrates.

GUESS WHAT? I set up cleaning stations on the reef, waiting for fish to stop by.

STARLING
SUPER SYNCHRONIZED

MY SQUAD IS CALLED a murmuration or flock. **I LIVE** in cities, parks, farms, and fields, and **I EAT** insects, berries, fruits, and seeds.

GUESS WHAT? I know where to fly by watching my closest seven neighbors.

KING PENGUIN
SUPER COLLABORATIVE

MY SQUAD IS CALLED a colony or rookery. **I LIVE** on the subantarctic islands, and **I EAT** squid and fish.

GUESS WHAT? It takes me about thirteen months to grow my waterproof feathers. During that time, I'm completely dependent on my parents for food.

Am I cuter than your stuffie?

VELVET WORM
SUPER SLY

MY SQUAD IS CALLED a cuddle. **I LIVE** in dark and humid places, like leaf litter and rotting wood, and **I EAT** small invertebrates, including crickets, spiders, and centipedes.

GUESS WHAT? Once I capture my prey, I bite into it and inject it with saliva, which liquefies its insides for easier eating.

Wiggle in to learn more!

CHILDREN'S BOOKS

Bunting, Philip. *The Wonderful Wisdom of Ants.* New York: Crown Books, 2020.

Coleman, Clara. *Whales Work Together.* New York: PowerKids, 2018.

Ellison, Nora. *Ants Work Together.* New York: PowerKids, 2018.

Fleming, Candace. *Honeybee: The Busy Life of Apis Mellifera.* Illustrated by Eric Rohmann. New York: Neal Porter, 2020.

Furrow, Robert, and Donna Jo Napoli. *We Are Starlings: Inside the Mesmerizing Magic of a Murmuration.* Illustrated by Marc Martin. New York: Random House Studio, 2023.

Henn, Sophy. *All Kinds of Animal Friends.* Tulsa, OK: Kane Miller, 2021.

Jacobson, Jennifer Richard. *Oh, Chickadee!* Illustrated by Jamie Hogan. Lincoln, ME: McSea, 2023.

Lindeen, Mary. *Dancing Bees and Other Amazing Communicators.* Minneapolis: Lerner, 2017.

Marsh, Laura. *Meerkats.* Washington, DC: National Geographic, 2013.

Poliquin, Rachel. *Beavers: The Superpower Field Guide.* Illustrated by Nicholas John Frith. Boston: Houghton Mifflin Harcourt, 2018.

Salyer, Hannah. *Packs: Strength in Numbers.* New York: Clarion Books, 2020.

Stamps, Caroline. *Animal Teams: How Amazing Animals Work Together in the Wild.* Illustrated by Charlotte Milner. New York: DK, 2022

ONLINE RESOURCES

"Black-Capped Chickadee." All About Birds, Cornell Lab of Ornithology. www.allaboutbirds.org/guide/Black-capped_Chickadee/overview#.

"King Penguin." National Geographic. www.nationalgeographic.com/animals/facts/king-penguin.

"Naked Mole-Rat." Animals, Small Mammal House, Smithsonian's National Zoo and Conservation Biology Institute. https://nationalzoo.si.edu/animals/naked-mole-rat.

Schueman, Lindsey Jean. "The Caste System and Gardening Proficiency of Leafcutter Ants." One Earth. www.oneearth.org/the-caste-system-and-gardening-proficiency-of-leafcutter-ants/.

"Unexpected Animal Pairings." BBC Earth. www.bbcearth.com/news/unexpected-animal-pairings.

"Watch: Bizarre Velvet Worms Shoot Slime Jets—Now We Know How." National Geographic. www.nationalgeographic.com/animals/article/150317-velvet-worms-animals-slime-science.

AUDIOVISUAL RESOURCES

Adventures of the Penguin King. Directed by Anthony Geffen and Sias Wilson. Atlantic Productions, 2013.

"Beaver Fever." Season 1, episode 2, of *Wild Hope* collection, *Nature.* Produced by Tangled Bank Studios. PBS, 2023.

"Finding the Way," "Homemaking," "Living Together," and "Friends and Rivals." Season 1, episodes 5, 6, 7, and 9, of *The Trials of Life.* Produced by Alistair Fothergill. BBC, 1990.

"The Incredible March of the Spiny Lobsters." Episode 36, *The Undersea World of Jacques Cousteau.* Produced by Jacques Cousteau. ABC, 1976.

Meerkat: A Dynasties Special. Directed by Emma Napper. BBC One, 2020.

Meerkat Manor. Seasons 1–4. Created and produced by Caroline Hawkins. Animal Planet, 2005–2008.

"Orca Dynasty." Season 1, episode 1, of *Secrets of the Whales.* Produced by James Cameron. National Geographic/Disney, 2021.

"Nature's Perfect Partners." Season 34, episode 15, of *Nature.* Produced by Sally Thomson. PBS, 2016.

Planet Ant: Life Inside the Colony. Directed and produced by Emma Napper. BBC Four, 2013.

"Snow Monkeys." Season 32, episode 16, of *Nature.* Written and produced by Joseph Pontecorvo. PBS, 2014.

"Spy in the Ocean: Deep Relationships." Season 42, episode 4, of *Nature.* Produced by John Downer. PBS, 2023.

AUTHORS' WEBSITES

Visit heatherlangbooks.com and jamieharper.com for additional resources and activities, including worksheets and links to videos of our supersquads in action.

ACKNOWLEDGMENTS

A special thank-you to the following experts, who not only confirmed and clarified facts but also provided us with rich details, which enhanced the text and illustrations in so many ways:

Dr. W. Randy Brooks, professor of biology, Florida Atlantic University; Peter E. Busher, professor emeritus, natural sciences and mathematics, Boston University; Dr. Mark J. Butler, professor and eminent scholar, Department of Biological Sciences, Florida International University; Dr. Chris Faulkes, evolutionary ecologist and naked mole rat researcher, Queen Mary University of London; Richard Gerum, postdoctoral researcher, York University; Dave Klinges, PhD student in ecology and conservation, University of Florida; Ian Magill, researcher at Harvard Medical School and at the Broad Institute of MIT and Harvard; Dr. Alex Thornton, professor of cognitive evolution, University of Exeter; and Dr. Thomas E. White, ARC DECRA fellow and senior lecturer, Sensory and Evolutionary Ecology (SEE) Lab, University of Sydney.

To Marty and Mary—
our super-duper friends and squadmates!
HL and JH

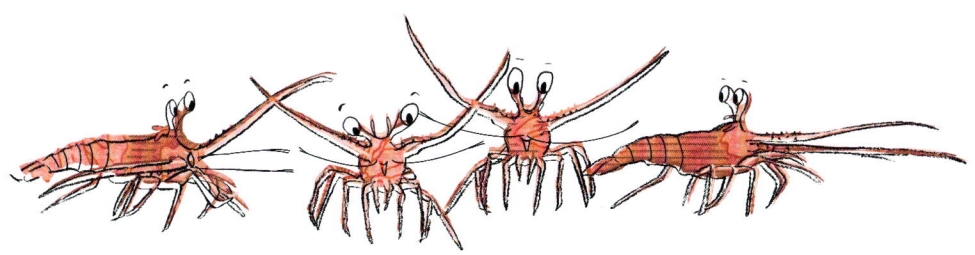

Text copyright © 2025 by Heather Lang and Jamie Harper
Illustrations copyright © 2025 by Jamie Harper

First edition 2025

Library of Congress Catalog Card Number pending
ISBN 978-1-5362-1798-8

25 26 27 28 29 30 CCP 10 9 8 7 6 5 4 3 2 1

Printed in Shenzhen, Guangdong, China

This book was typeset in Futura.
The illustrations were done using traditional and digital collage.

Candlewick Press
99 Dover Street
Somerville, Massachusetts 02144

www.candlewick.com

EU Authorized Representative: HackettFlynn Ltd, 36 Cloch Choirneal,
Balrothery, Co. Dublin, K32 C942, Ireland. EU@walkerpublishinggroup.com